EMMANUEL JOSEPH

The Diplomats' Labyrinth: Navigating Global Politics

Copyright © 2025 by Emmanuel Joseph

All rights reserved. No part of this publication may be reproduced, stored or transmitted in any form or by any means, electronic, mechanical, photocopying, recording, scanning, or otherwise without written permission from the publisher. It is illegal to copy this book, post it to a website, or distribute it by any other means without permission.

First edition

This book was professionally typeset on Reedsy.
Find out more at reedsy.com

Contents

1. Chapter 1 — 1
2. Chapter 1: The First Steps into Diplomacy — 2
3. Chapter 2: The Art of Negotiation — 4
4. Chapter 3: The Power of Cultural Diplomacy — 6
5. Chapter 4: Crisis Management in Diplomacy — 9
6. Chapter 5: Building Alliances and Partnerships — 11
7. Chapter 6: Diplomacy in the Digital Age — 13
8. Chapter 7: Environmental Diplomacy — 15
9. Chapter 8: The Role of Economic Diplomacy — 17
10. Chapter 9: Humanitarian Diplomacy — 19
11. Chapter 10: Public Diplomacy and Soft Power — 21
12. Chapter 11: Women in Diplomacy — 23
13. Chapter 12: Reflections on Diplomacy — 25

Chapter 1

The Diplomats' Labyrinth: Navigating Global Politics

2

Chapter 1: The First Steps into Diplomacy

Embarking on the journey of diplomacy often begins with a simple yet profound realization—the world is a tapestry of cultures, each thread representing a unique perspective. As a young diplomat, Maria Alvarez learned this firsthand when she was stationed in Cairo. Her initial months were a whirlwind of cultural immersion, learning the local customs, and building relationships. These experiences taught her that diplomacy is not just about politics; it's about understanding the human element behind every handshake. Through countless tea ceremonies and discussions, Maria discovered that empathy and respect are the foundation of effective diplomacy.

In the heart of Cairo, Maria faced her first diplomatic challenge—a trade dispute that threatened to sour relations between Egypt and Spain. With patience and perseverance, she navigated the labyrinth of political intricacies, balancing her country's interests with the need for a harmonious resolution. Her mentor, Ambassador Hassan, advised her to listen more than she spoke, a lesson that would become her guiding principle. The resolution of the dispute marked Maria's first major success, earning her respect and recognition among her peers.

Maria's journey in Cairo was also marked by personal growth. She forged

CHAPTER 1: THE FIRST STEPS INTO DIPLOMACY

friendships with local diplomats, learning to appreciate the beauty of Arabic poetry and the intricacies of Egyptian cuisine. These experiences enriched her understanding of the region's culture, making her a more effective diplomat. The lessons she learned in Cairo would serve as a foundation for her future endeavors, shaping her approach to diplomacy in ways she could never have imagined.

As Maria's tenure in Cairo came to an end, she reflected on the transformative journey she had undertaken. She had arrived as a novice, unsure of her place in the world of diplomacy, but she left with a deep sense of purpose and a commitment to bridging divides. Her experiences in Egypt were a testament to the power of cultural exchange and the importance of building relationships based on mutual respect and understanding.

3

Chapter 2: The Art of Negotiation

Negotiation is the heart and soul of diplomacy, and for seasoned diplomat Li Wei, it is an art form. His years of experience taught him that successful negotiations require a delicate balance of firmness and flexibility. In a highstakes negotiation between China and the United States over trade tariffs, Li faced one of his greatest challenges. The stakes were high, and the pressure was immense, but Li's calm demeanor and strategic thinking allowed him to navigate the complexities of the talks.

Li understood that every word and gesture carried weight. He meticulously prepared for each session, anticipating the arguments and counterarguments that would be presented. His ability to remain composed under pressure earned him the respect of his American counterparts. Through a series of intense discussions, both sides gradually moved closer to a mutually beneficial agreement. Li's expertise in finding common ground and his commitment to a fair outcome were instrumental in reaching a resolution.

The negotiation process also highlighted the importance of trust and rapport. Li's counterpart, Ambassador Smith, recognized the value of Li's integrity and transparency. This mutual respect fostered an environment where both parties felt comfortable expressing their concerns and priorities. It was through this collaborative approach that they were able to overcome the

CHAPTER 2: THE ART OF NEGOTIATION

hurdles and find a solution that satisfied both nations' interests.

In the aftermath of the successful negotiation, Li reflected on the lessons he had learned. He understood that negotiation was not just about securing favorable terms but also about building lasting relationships. The trust and respect that were cultivated during the talks laid the groundwork for future cooperation between the two countries. Li's experience underscored the significance of diplomacy in fostering global stability and prosperity.

4

Chapter 3: The Power of Cultural Diplomacy

Cultural diplomacy is a powerful tool in the arsenal of any diplomat. It transcends political boundaries and connects people on a deeper level. For Ambassador Amina Malik, cultural diplomacy became her primary focus during her tenure in Paris. She believed that art, music, and literature had the potential to bridge divides and foster mutual understanding. Her efforts in promoting cultural exchange between Pakistan and France led to a remarkable transformation in bilateral relations.

Amina organized a series of cultural events that showcased the rich heritage of Pakistan. From art exhibitions to musical performances, these events captivated the French audience and sparked a newfound interest in Pakistani culture. The highlight of her efforts was a collaborative art project involving artists from both countries. This initiative not only fostered creativity but also created lasting bonds between the participants.

Through cultural diplomacy, Amina also addressed misconceptions and stereotypes. She engaged in dialogues that explored the commonalities between the two cultures, highlighting shared values and traditions. These discussions were instrumental in breaking down barriers and fostering a sense of unity. Amina's work demonstrated that cultural diplomacy could be a powerful force for positive change, promoting peace and understanding in an increasingly interconnected world.

The impact of Amina's efforts extended beyond the realm of culture. Her initiatives paved the way for enhanced economic and political cooperation between Pakistan and France. The cultural exchange programs created opportunities for collaboration in various sectors, from tourism to education. Amina's legacy as a diplomat was defined by her ability to harness the power of culture to build bridges and create lasting connections.

The role of culture in diplomacy is often underestimated. Yet, cultural diplomacy is a powerful tool in building bridges between nations. It is through cultural exchanges, art, music, and traditions that countries can connect on a deeper, more personal level. Diplomats who harness the power of culture can open doors that would otherwise remain closed, creating opportunities for dialogue and understanding.

Cultural diplomacy requires a deep appreciation and understanding of the diverse cultures that populate our world. Diplomats must immerse themselves in the customs, traditions, and values of the countries they engage with. This cultural sensitivity allows them to navigate complex social landscapes, building trust and rapport with their counterparts. It is through this understanding that diplomats can find common ground, even in the most challenging of situations.

One of the most effective forms of cultural diplomacy is the exchange of art and literature. Artistic expressions transcend language barriers and touch the hearts of people. Through exhibitions, performances, and literary exchanges, diplomats can showcase their nation's cultural heritage while also celebrating the richness of other cultures. These cultural exchanges foster mutual respect and admiration, laying the groundwork for more formal diplomatic engagements.

Education and academic exchanges are another vital aspect of cultural diplomacy. By promoting educational opportunities and academic collaborations, diplomats can build lasting relationships between future leaders and scholars. These exchanges create networks of individuals who are invested in understanding and solving global challenges together. It is through these educational ties that countries can cultivate a sense of shared responsibility and cooperation.

Cultural diplomacy is not without its challenges. It requires patience, open-mindedness, and a genuine desire to learn from others. Diplomatic efforts can be hindered by cultural misunderstandings or biases. However, seasoned diplomats understand that the rewards of cultural diplomacy far outweigh the risks. By embracing the richness of cultural diversity, diplomats can pave the way for a more interconnected and harmonious world.

5

Chapter 4: Crisis Management in Diplomacy

Crises are an inevitable part of the diplomatic landscape, and the ability to manage them effectively is a hallmark of seasoned diplomats. For Ambassador James Carter, crisis management became a defining aspect of his career. During his tenure in Tokyo, he faced a series of challenges that tested his skills and resilience. From natural disasters to geopolitical tensions, James navigated each crisis with a steady hand and a clear vision.

The earthquake that struck Japan during James' tenure was one of the most significant crises he encountered. The devastation was immense, and the immediate priority was to coordinate relief efforts. James worked tirelessly to facilitate international aid, liaising with governments and organizations to ensure that assistance reached those in need. His leadership during this critical period earned him the admiration of both his colleagues and the Japanese people.

In the aftermath of the earthquake, James focused on longterm recovery efforts. He recognized the importance of rebuilding not just infrastructure but also trust and hope. Through diplomatic channels, he facilitated partnerships between Japan and other countries, fostering collaboration in areas such as disaster preparedness and technological innovation. James' efforts contributed to the resilience and recovery of the affected communities, leaving a lasting impact on the region.

Geopolitical tensions also tested James' crisis management skills. During a diplomatic standoff between Japan and a neighboring country, he played a pivotal role in deescalating the situation. Through careful negotiation and strategic communication, James was able to diffuse tensions and pave the way for a peaceful resolution. His ability to remain calm under pressure and his commitment to finding diplomatic solutions were key to his success.

6

Chapter 5: Building Alliances and Partnerships

Building alliances and partnerships is a cornerstone of effective diplomacy. Ambassador Rania Hussein's tenure in Berlin was marked by her efforts to strengthen ties between Egypt and Germany. She believed that collaboration in areas such as trade, education, and technology could lead to mutual prosperity. Rania's diplomatic acumen and strategic vision enabled her to forge strong alliances that benefitted both nations.

Rania's first major achievement was the establishment of a bilateral trade agreement that opened new avenues for economic cooperation. Through extensive consultations and negotiations, she ensured that the agreement addressed the priorities and concerns of both countries. The successful implementation of the agreement led to increased trade and investment, creating opportunities for businesses and entrepreneurs.

Education was another area where Rania focused her efforts. She initiated student exchange programs that allowed young people from Egypt and Germany to experience each other's cultures and educational systems. These programs fostered mutual understanding and created a new generation of global citizens with a deep appreciation for diverse perspectives. Rania's work in this area demonstrated the transformative power of education in building bridges between nations.

Technology and innovation were also central to Rania's diplomatic agenda. She facilitated partnerships between research institutions and technology companies, fostering collaboration on cuttingedge projects. These initiatives led to advancements in areas such as renewable energy and sustainable development. Rania's ability to identify and capitalize on opportunities for collaboration made her a respected and influential figure in the diplomatic community.

7

Chapter 6: Diplomacy in the Digital Age

The digital age has transformed the landscape of diplomacy, creating new opportunities and challenges for diplomats. Ambassador Alejandro Martinez embraced these changes during his tenure in London, leveraging technology to enhance diplomatic efforts. He recognized that digital diplomacy could amplify traditional diplomatic practices and create new channels for engagement.

Alejandro's first major initiative was the creation of a digital platform that facilitated communication between diplomats and the public. Through social media and online forums, he engaged with citizens, addressing their concerns and sharing insights on diplomatic efforts. This approach not only increased transparency but also fostered a sense of inclusivity. Alejandro's use of digital tools made diplomacy more accessible and relatable to the general public.

In addition to public engagement, Alejandro also utilized technology to enhance diplomatic negotiations. He implemented secure video conferencing systems that allowed for realtime communication between diplomats in different countries. This innovation streamlined the negotiation process, enabling more efficient and effective discussions. Alejandro's efforts demonstrated the potential of technology to bridge geographical divides and facilitate diplomatic collaboration.

Cybersecurity was another area where Alejandro focused his efforts. He recognized the growing threat of cyberattacks and worked to develop strategies for protecting diplomatic communications and sensitive information. Through partnerships with tech companies and cybersecurity experts, Alejandro implemented measures to safeguard diplomatic operations. His proactive approach to cybersecurity highlighted the importance of adapting diplomatic practices to the digital age.

8

Chapter 7: Environmental Diplomacy

development. Sofia's ability to bring together diverse stakeholders and foster constructive dialogue was key to the conference's success. Her work demonstrated the importance of collective action in addressing environmental challenges.

Sofia also focused on promoting sustainable practices at the grassroots level. She supported communitybased initiatives that aimed to protect natural resources and promote environmental stewardship. By empowering local communities, Sofia helped create a network of environmental advocates who were committed to making a difference. Her efforts highlighted the role of diplomacy in driving environmental sustainability and resilience.

In addition to her work on climate change, Sofia addressed issues related to biodiversity and conservation. She collaborated with international organizations to develop strategies for protecting endangered species and preserving natural habitats. Through these partnerships, Sofia helped raise awareness about the importance of biodiversity and the need for global cooperation in conservation efforts.

Sofia's legacy as an environmental diplomat was defined by her dedication to finding sustainable solutions and her ability to inspire others to take action.

Her work in Nairobi demonstrated the power of diplomacy to address some of the most pressing challenges of our time and create a more sustainable future for all.

9

Chapter 8: The Role of Economic Diplomacy

Economic diplomacy is a crucial aspect of international relations, and Ambassador Michael Johnson's tenure in Brussels was marked by his efforts to promote economic cooperation between the European Union and the United States. Michael believed that fostering strong economic ties could lead to greater prosperity and stability for both regions.

One of Michael's key achievements was the negotiation of a comprehensive trade agreement that aimed to reduce barriers to trade and investment. Through extensive consultations and negotiations, Michael worked to ensure that the agreement addressed the interests of both parties. The successful implementation of the agreement led to increased trade and investment, creating new opportunities for businesses and entrepreneurs on both sides of the Atlantic.

Michael also focused on promoting innovation and technology as drivers of economic growth. He facilitated partnerships between research institutions and technology companies, fostering collaboration on cuttingedge projects. These initiatives led to advancements in areas such as artificial intelligence, renewable energy, and healthcare. Michael's work demonstrated the potential of economic diplomacy to drive technological progress and improve the quality of life for people around the world.

In addition to his work on trade and technology, Michael addressed issues related to economic development and poverty reduction. He supported initiatives that aimed to create jobs, improve infrastructure, and enhance education and healthcare services. Through these efforts, Michael helped promote inclusive economic growth and reduce inequalities, contributing to greater social and economic stability.

Michael's legacy as an economic diplomat was defined by his commitment to fostering economic cooperation and his ability to identify and capitalize on opportunities for collaboration. His work in Brussels demonstrated the transformative power of economic diplomacy in promoting prosperity and stability.

10

Chapter 9: Humanitarian Diplomacy

Humanitarian diplomacy is a vital aspect of international relations, and Ambassador Fatima Nasser's work in Amman exemplified this role. During her tenure, she dedicated herself to addressing the humanitarian crises that affected the region, including the refugee crisis and natural disasters. Fatima believed that diplomacy could play a crucial role in alleviating human suffering and promoting peace.

Fatima's first major initiative was the establishment of a humanitarian aid program that provided assistance to refugees and displaced persons. She worked closely with international organizations, governments, and NGOs to coordinate relief efforts and ensure that aid reached those in need. Fatima's leadership and dedication to the cause earned her the respect and admiration of her colleagues and the people she served.

In addition to providing immediate relief, Fatima focused on longterm solutions to the humanitarian crises. She supported initiatives that aimed to improve access to education, healthcare, and livelihood opportunities for refugees and displaced persons. Through these efforts, Fatima helped create a path to selfsufficiency and empowerment for vulnerable populations.

Fatima also addressed the root causes of the humanitarian crises by advocating for conflict resolution and peacebuilding efforts. She worked tirelessly to facilitate dialogue between conflicting parties, promoting peaceful solutions and fostering reconciliation. Her ability to bring together diverse stakeholders and foster constructive dialogue was key to her success in this area.

Fatima's legacy as a humanitarian diplomat was defined by her compassion, dedication, and ability to inspire others to take action. Her work in Amman demonstrated the power of diplomacy to address some of the most pressing humanitarian challenges of our time and create a more just and peaceful world.

11

Chapter 10: Public Diplomacy and Soft Power

Public diplomacy and soft power are essential tools for diplomats seeking to influence global public opinion and build positive relationships with other countries. Ambassador Julia Kim's tenure in Seoul was marked by her innovative approach to public diplomacy, which emphasized cultural exchange, communication, and engagement with the public.

Julia's first major initiative was the launch of a cultural exchange program that aimed to promote mutual understanding and appreciation between South Korea and other countries. She organized cultural events, including art exhibitions, film festivals, and music performances, that showcased the rich heritage of South Korea. These events captivated audiences and sparked a newfound interest in Korean culture, contributing to a positive image of the country on the global stage.

In addition to cultural exchange, Julia focused on engaging with the public through social media and online platforms. She recognized the importance of digital communication in shaping public opinion and used these tools to share insights on diplomatic efforts and address misconceptions. Julia's use of social media made diplomacy more accessible and relatable to the general public, fostering a sense of inclusivity and transparency.

Julia also addressed issues related to soft power, including the promotion of education and language learning. She supported initiatives that aimed to increase the number of students studying abroad and learning foreign languages. Through these efforts, Julia helped create a new generation of global citizens with a deep appreciation for diverse perspectives and cultures.

Julia's legacy as a public diplomat was defined by her innovative approach to diplomacy and her ability to connect with people on a personal level. Her work in Seoul demonstrated the power of public diplomacy and soft power in shaping global public opinion and building positive relationships between countries.

12

Chapter 11: Women in Diplomacy

The role of women in diplomacy has evolved significantly over the years, and Ambassador Elena Rodriguez's career is a testament to this progress. During her tenure in Buenos Aires, Elena dedicated herself to promoting gender equality and empowering women in the field of diplomacy. She believed that diverse perspectives and inclusive practices were essential for effective diplomacy.

Elena's first major initiative was the establishment of a mentorship program for young female diplomats. She recognized the importance of providing support and guidance to the next generation of women in diplomacy. Through this program, Elena helped create a network of female diplomats who could share their experiences, challenges, and successes. The program not only empowered young women but also fostered a sense of solidarity and community.

In addition to mentorship, Elena advocated for policies that promoted gender equality within diplomatic institutions. She worked to ensure that women had equal opportunities for career advancement and representation in decisionmaking positions. Elena's efforts led to significant changes within her organization, including the implementation of gendersensitive policies and practices.

Elena also focused on promoting women's rights and gender equality on the global stage. She used her platform as a diplomat to raise awareness about issues such as genderbased violence, women's economic empowerment, and access to education and healthcare. Through her advocacy, Elena helped create a more inclusive and equitable world for women and girls.

Elena's legacy as a diplomat was defined by her dedication to promoting gender equality and empowering women. Her work in Buenos Aires demonstrated the importance of diversity and inclusion in diplomacy and the significant contributions that women can make to the field.

13

Chapter 12: Reflections on Diplomacy

The world of diplomacy is everchanging, and each diplomat's journey is unique. Ambassador David Nguyen's career, spanning several decades and continents, is a reflection of the evolving nature of diplomacy. During his tenure, David faced numerous challenges and triumphs, each experience contributing to his growth as a diplomat.

David's first posting was in Nairobi, where he encountered the complexities of international relations and the importance of cultural understanding. His experiences in Kenya taught him the value of empathy and respect in diplomacy. As he progressed in his career, David's assignments took him to various parts of the world, each with its own set of challenges and opportunities.

One of David's most significant accomplishments was his role in facilitating peace negotiations in a conflictridden region. Through his unwavering commitment to finding a peaceful resolution, David helped bring an end to years of violence and suffering. His ability to navigate the intricacies of the peace process and build trust among conflicting parties was instrumental in achieving a lasting agreement.

As David reflected on his career, he recognized the importance of adaptability and continuous learning in diplomacy. He understood that the world was constantly changing, and diplomats needed to evolve with it. David's experiences underscored the significance of diplomacy in promoting global stability, peace, and prosperity.

David's legacy as a diplomat was defined by his dedication to fostering understanding and cooperation among nations. His career demonstrated the transformative power of diplomacy and the impact that dedicated individuals can have on the world stage. Through his reflections, David hoped to inspire future generations of diplomats to embrace the challenges and opportunities of this noble profession.

www.ingramcontent.com/pod-product-compliance
Lightning Source LLC
LaVergne TN
LVHW010445070526
838199LV00066B/6196